Rockets

MY SISTER'S NAME IS ROVER

Rover Goes to School

Chris Powling and Scoular Anderson

A & C Black • London

Rockets

ROVER

Chris Powling & Scoular Anderson

Rover's Birthday
Rover the Champion
Rover Goes to School
Rover Shows Off

Published 1999 by A & C Black (Publishers) Ltd
35 Bedford Row, London WC1R 4JH

Text copyright © 1999 Chris Powling
Illustrations copyright © 1999 Scoular Anderson

The right of Chris Powling and Scoular Anderson to be
identified as author and illustrator of this work has
been asserted by them in accordance with the
Copyright, Designs and Patents Act 1988.

ISBN 0-7136-5197-0

A CIP catalogue record for this book is available
from the British Library.

Printed and bound by G. Z. Printek, Bilbao, Spain.

My sister's name is Rover... okay?

She won't answer if you call her anything else. She just points to the puppy costume Granpa made for her.

My sister sleeps in the puppy costume.

She eats in the puppy costume.

She goes for walks in the puppy
costume... mostly on a lead with me
holding the other end.

'You're her brother, Barney,' Mum says.
'It's the sort of thing brothers do.'
Thanks, Mum.

And when the puppy costume is being washed, my sister just sits and mopes.

She was moping under the washing line one Sunday morning when grumpy Mrs Robinson from next door looked over her fence.

Mrs Robinson's face turned pink.

'You've put your new puppy in the washing machine?' she gasped. 'And now you've pegged it out on the washing line?'

She hurried indoors muttering under her breath.

But by Monday morning the puppy
costume was dry and Rover was back
in action.

I couldn't believe it.

It was true, though. Mum and Dad had agreed to it.

Dad had written a note:

Cherry Orchard Cottage
Falstaff Street
Globeston

<u>Mon</u>.

Dear Mr Goodwin,

Would you let Sara wear her puppy costume to school for the day? Granpa made it as a present — I'm sure you'll understand. Barney will keep an eye on her. Many thanks.

Jon Bornden

14

Things were going from bad to worse.

So I took Rover to school.
Mr Lucas, the crossing man,
nearly dropped his lollipop.
'Good morning, Barney.
Good morning... er...'

16

As she crossed the road, Rover waved
and blew kisses at everyone.

All the kids and all the traffic came to a complete standstill. It was as if a rock singer or a famous footballer was visiting the school.

When we finally made it into school,
I headed straight for the head teacher's
office to give him Dad's note. Surely
Mr Goodwin would see sense.

But even he seemed pleased to see us.
'Okay, Barney,' he grinned. 'We'll let
your sister off school uniform just
this once.'

I ask you.

Would you like to spend a day in class
with a kid sister in a puppy costume?

Now I was really embarrassed. What would my class teacher say about it? Her name is Mrs Duggan. The Dragon is what we call her.

You'll hate your new teacher, Rover, with any luck.

The Dragon let us read our favourite Michael Rosen poems out loud. I chose one about a dog.

At this, my sister wagged her tail like
mad. And Mrs Duggan actually smiled.

Here's the one I wrote first of all:

Down among the dustbins
I met a dog called Rover.
She's such a stinky
show-off though,
I wish today was over.

This wasn't quite what The Dragon
wanted, of course. So I crossed it out
and wrote another one:

Down behind the dustbins
I met a dog called Rover.
She's such a mighty mega-star
I call her Super-Nova.

'Super-Nova?' someone said. 'What kind of name is that?'

'It's a star that gets brighter and brighter,' said Mrs Duggan. 'So it fits our little friend here perfectly.'
Then she turned to me.

It's lovely to see a boy who's so brotherly, Barney.

Brotherly?

I'd have divorced my little sister if I could.

In Maths we measured her.

In Science we studied two clusters of stars called The Dog Stars.

And at storytime, Mrs Duggan even
began reading a book called 'WOOF!'.

Out in the playground
after lunch, I thought
all the other Infants
would pat my sister
to death.

By now I'd written another poem in my head:

Down behind the dustbins
I met a dog called Rover.
I thought that school might cure her
But she took the whole place over.

Maybe the afternoon would
be different I told myself.

No chance.

Can you guess who
we drew in the
Art lesson?

Or which of us was best at PE?

No wonder Rover was exhausted
when it came to assembly time
at the end of the afternoon.
In the Hall, she curled up
beside me sleepily.

First Mr Goodwin told us about the
Summer Fete on Saturday.

Then he introduced a special
visitor. 'This is Caroline from the LOOK
AFTER ANIMALS SOCIETY,' he said.

35

Caroline nodded. She was a tiny lady with smiley eyes. Except now they looked rather sad.

She waited till everyone was quiet.

Caroline gave us all a serious look. 'Why only yesterday I had a terrible phone call,' she said. 'The lady who made it was so upset she forgot to leave her name and address.'

Everyone gasped.

Caroline looked
ready to burst
into tears.

Suddenly...

My sister bounded down to the front so fast I could hardly keep up with her.

'Er... this is Rover,' said Mr Goodwin.
'And her brother, Barney. Their parents
are actors, Caroline – and their Granpa
made that puppy costume.'

He stared hard at my sister.

Rover acted the whole thing out,
with a bit of help from me.
She used a drama-block
as the washing machine...

She used a skipping rope as the washing line and pegs from the display.

And she borrowed Mr Goodwin's glasses to help her play Mrs Robinson.

Soon everyone was laughing their heads off. 'Oh dear,' said Caroline, wiping her eyes. 'I don't get many jokes in my job.'

She finished her talk with my sister stretched out at her feet.

At the end, everyone clapped loudly.
Then somebody shouted, 'Three cheers
for Rover and Caroline!'

I think it may have been me.

Mind you, I'll leave Granpa to explain things to Mrs Robinson.

The End